I'm and Won't, They're and Don't

What's a Contraction?

To Tresa, Kelly, Clare, and Shannon
—B.P.C.

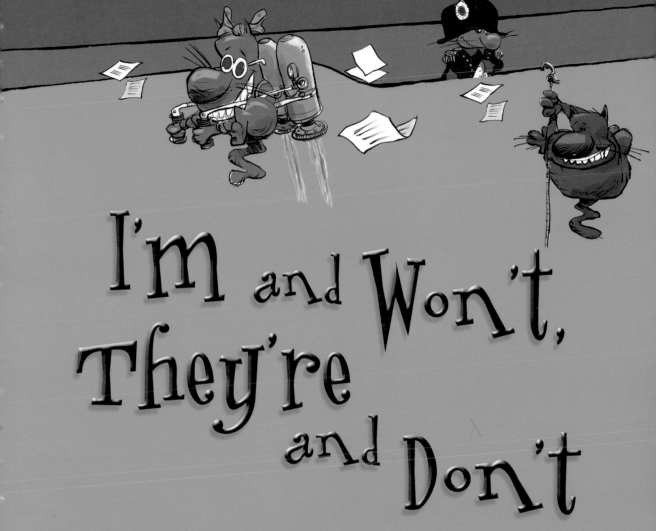

I'm and Won't, They're and Don't

What's a Contraction?

by Brian P. Cleary

illustrations by Brian Gable

M MILLBROOK PRESS / MINNEAPOLIS

contractions
take a couple words
or sometimes even three

SHE IS

and shrink them
into only one,
as in, "She's drinking tea."

"She's" is the contraction,

and it shortens up "she is."

It takes two words
and makes them one,

as in, "That's mine and his."

As punctuation goes,
contractions always
feature these:

They take the place of letters, and they're called apostrophes.

Take a phrase like "does not."

A contraction makes it "doesn't."

Try another: "Was not."
You can shorten it to "wasn't."

Apostrophes help link the words and replace at least one letter.

As in, "I'm very proud that I've helped make this lovely sweater."

oftentimes contractions
join another word to "not."

Like "shouldn't it be colder now?"

and "can't I take your spot?"

"I don't think this shoe is mine."

"Isn't it absurd?"

THEY'RE WE'LL
SHE'S I'D
CAN'T COULDN'T
I'LL

All these turn a
two-word phrase
into one single word.

other times, contractions shorten "are" or "is" or "am."

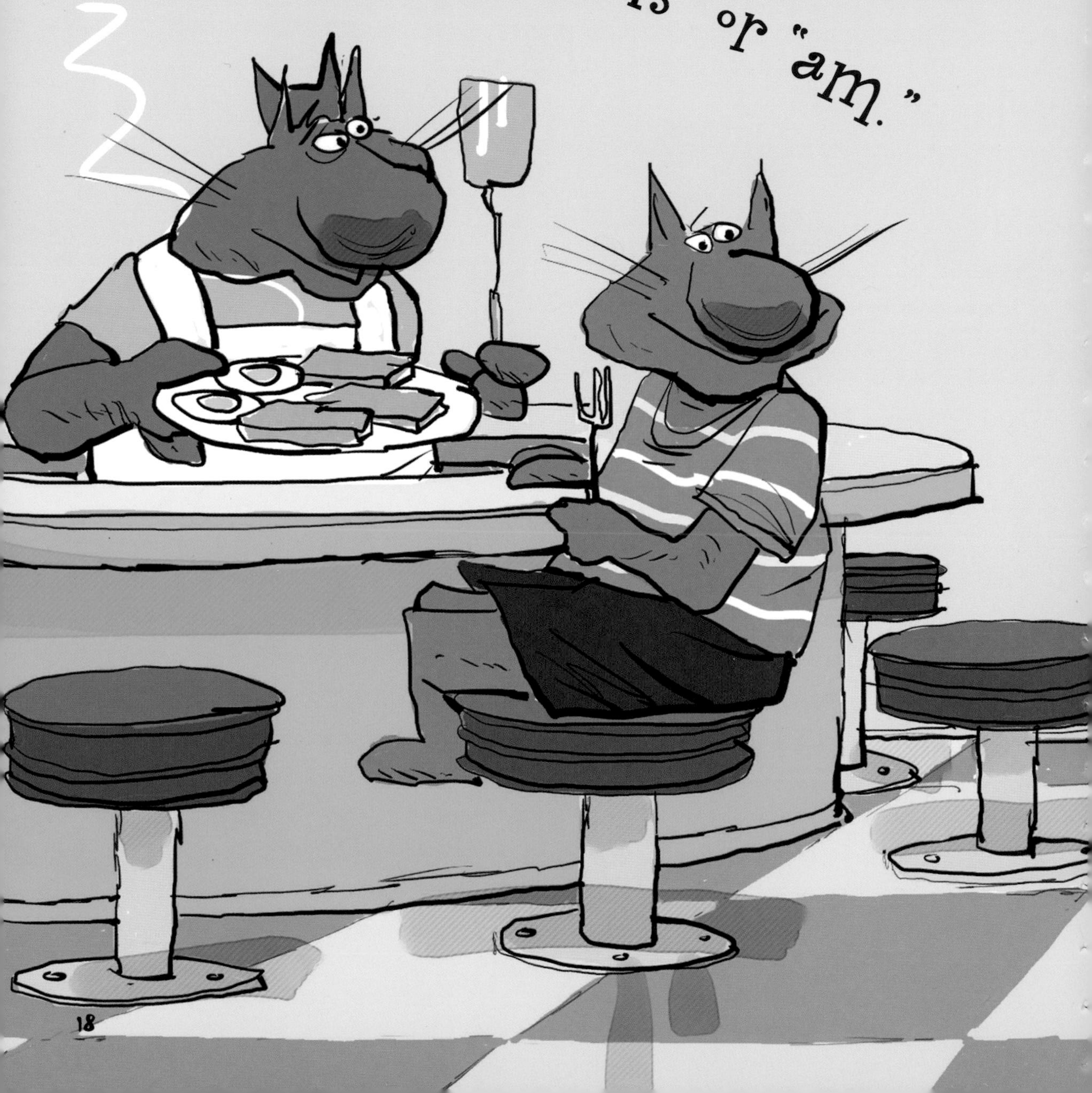

Now and then, contractions shorten not just two . . .

but three words, for example,
"I'd've thought this was the zoo!"

"Would" when it's contracted
is reduced to just a "d"

in words like "I'd" and "she'd"

as well as "you'd"
to name just three.

"Will" can come in handy as a future-tense contraction.

Shrink "she will"
right down to "she'll"—
it's smaller by a fraction.

Sometimes you'll find "have" and "had" have been abbreviated.

Like here: "I've got a puppy," and "I'd better get him crated."

Aren't contractions useful words? In speech and writing

have any fear
in using them.

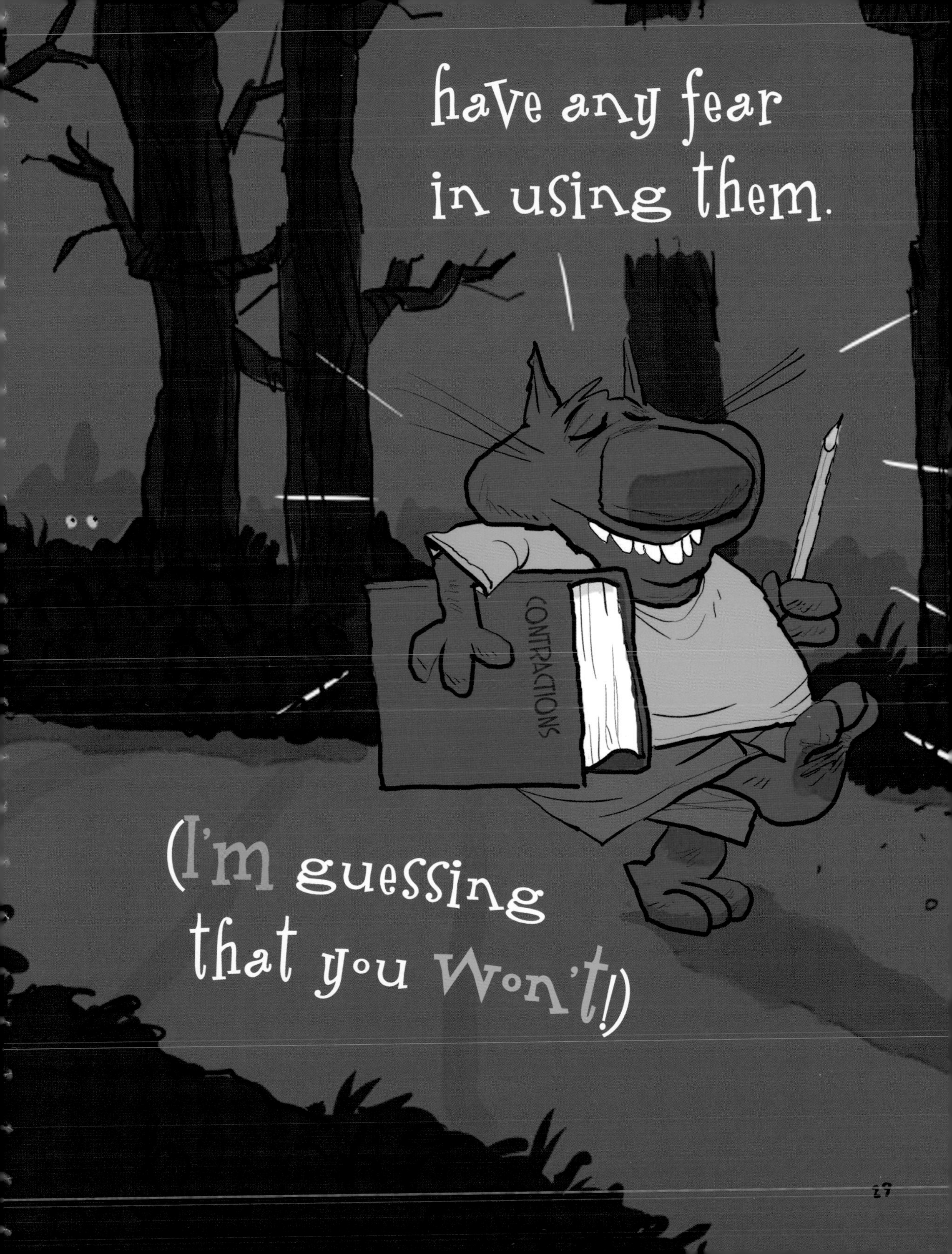

(I'm guessing
that you won't!)

So What's a contraction?

Do you know?

Find activities, games, and more at
www.brianpcleary.com

ABOUT THE AUTHOR & ILLUSTRATOR

BRIAN P. CLEARY is the author of the best-selling *Words Are CATegorical®* series as well as the *Math Is CATegorical®*, *Food Is CATegorical™*, *Adventures in Memory™*, and *Sounds Like Reading®* series. He has also written <u>The Punctuation Station</u>, <u>The Laugh Stand: Adventures in Humor</u>, and several other books. He lives in Cleveland, Ohio.

BRIAN GABLE is the illustrator of many *Words Are CATegorical®* books and the *Math Is CATegorical®* series. Mr. Gable also works as a political cartoonist for the <u>Globe and Mail</u> newspaper in Toronto, Canada.

Millbrook Press
A division of Lerner Publishing Group, Inc.
241 First Avenue North
Minneapolis, MN 55401 U.S.A.

Website address: www.lernerbooks.com

Library of Congress Cataloging-in-Publication Data

Cleary, Brian P., 1959—
    I'm and won't, they're and don't : what's a contraction? / by Brian P. Cleary ; illustrated by Brian Gable.
      p.   cm. — (Words are CATegorical)
    ISBN: 978—0—8225—9155—9 (lib. bdg. : alk. paper)
    1. English language—Contraction—Juvenile literature. 2. Contraction—Juvenile literature. 3. Language arts (Primary) I. Gable, Brian, 1949— ill. II. Title.
PE1161.C54 2010
421'.54—dc22   2009049201

Manufactured in the United States of America
1 — DP — 7/15/10